Therapy Pets

Jill Eckersley is a freelance writer with ~~~~ ~~~~~~ ~~~~~~~~~~ ~~~~~~~ ~~g on
~~~~~~ ~~~~~ ~~~~ ~~~~~~~ ~~~~~ terest
~~~~~ ~~~~~~~ ~~~~~~ ~~~~~~~ titles.

Dennistoun Library
2a Craigpark
Glasgow G31 2NA
Phone: 0141 276 0768

~~~~~~ *oping*
~~~~~~ *nan's*
~~~~~~ *oping*
~~~~~~ Aziz)
lives

This book is due for return on or before the last date shown below. It may be
renewed by telephone, personal application, fax or post, quoting this date,
author, title and the book number.

Overcoming Common Problems Series

Selected titles

A full list of titles is available from Sheldon Press,
36 Causton Street, London SW1P 4ST and on our website at
www.sheldonpress.co.uk

Therapy Pets

a guide

Jill Eckersley

sheldon PRESS

First published in Great Britain in 2016

Sheldon Press
36 Causton Street
London SW1P 4ST
www.sheldonpress.co.uk

The author and publisher have made every effort to ensure that the
external website and email addresses included in this book are correct and
up to date at the time of going to press. The author and publisher are not
responsible for the content, quality or continuing accessibility of the sites.

British Library Cataloguing-in-Publication Data
A catalogue record for this book is available from the British Library

ISBN 978-1-84709-409-4
eBook ISBN 978-1-84709-410-0

Typeset by Fakenham Prepress Solutions, Fakenham, Norfolk NR21 8NN
First printed in Great Britain by Ashford Colour Press
Subsequently digitally reprinted in Great Britain

eBook by Fakenham Prepress Solutions, Fakenham, Norfolk NR21 8NN

Produced on paper from sustainable forests

*To the staff and volunteers
of the Mayhew Animal Home,
with thanks for Mo!*

Contents

Acknowledgements

So many people – and animals – have both inspired and helped me with this book. Bronwen Gray of The Retreat, Sallie Bolland of Stroke Rehab Dogs, James Bowen and Street Cat Bob, author Jacki Gordon, Sue McAlister of the NI Prison Service, Annie Sinnott of the Old Vicarage Care Home, Luke Berman of the Mayhew Animal Home, Amy Wilton and Holly the Whippet, Toni Brown-Griffin and Hetty, Dinah Baynton-Dibley from PAT, Jayne Dillon, Lorcan and Jessi-Cat, Harriet from the Ian Mikardo High School and McFlurry, Belinda Johnston from Our Special Friends, Suzi Cretney from the Donkey Sanctuary and Bee Pike from the Wormwood Scrubs Pony Centre. Thank you all.

1

How pet therapy began . . .

When you come home after a difficult day at work, there's nothing better than a tail-wagging canine to cheer you up and seem pleased to see you – unless it's a snoozing feline purring gently on the sofa as if to remind you that nothing is really *that* bad!

Animal lovers feel instinctively that pets are good for us, but could there be some scientific truth in this? It seems that there could. After all, early man often depended on signals from animals for survival – suggesting either that he and his family were safe, or that there was some sort of threat out there. There's evidence from the ancient world that dogs, for instance, were treasured family members even before writing was invented. A 12,000-year-old grave was excavated in Ein Mallala, Israel, that revealed the remains of an elderly man with his arms round a puppy. The Ancient Egyptians shaved their eyebrows as a sign of mourning when their pet dogs or cats died. Dog saliva was considered medicinal as it was observed that dogs' wounds healed up after they had licked them. And Roman ladies carried lap-dogs, which were supposed to soothe stomach-ache.

The first recorded use of animals as therapy for sick humans was recorded at Gheel in Belgium in the ninth century, when people with disabilities were encouraged to care for animals in order to 're-establish the harmony of soul and body'.

In our own time, something called the 'biophilia hypothesis', described by the distinguished American biologist and researcher Edward O. Wilson in a book of the same name in 1984, suggests that there is an instinctive bond between human beings and other living things. It would explain why most of us are drawn to appealing mammals – especially young ones – and why we choose to care for, and even risk our lives on behalf of, both domestic and wild creatures.

Dogs, horses and farm animals such as oxen have worked along-side humans for millennia. At the end of the eighteenth century another small step was taken towards what we now call 'pet therapy' when a Quaker businessman and philanthropist from Yorkshire named William Tuke, appalled by the cruel and primitive conditions he witnessed in his local 'lunatic asylum', decided that animals could play a part in treating people with mental illness. He raised funds through his Quaker connections and in 1796 he opened The Retreat, a facility where mentally ill people could be cared for in a much more humane and enlightened way. He felt that looking after both farm animals and small domestic pets would 'awaken the social and benevolent feelings' of patients. Rabbits, seagulls and hawks were introduced as pets.

Tuke's ideas spread around Europe. Doctors at an institution for people with epilepsy in Bielefeld, Germany, began to allow the patients to look after sheep, horses and monkeys and noted that this treatment left women patients 'cheerfully enlightened' and enabled male patients to tell their troubles to dogs and cats.

Like the Bethel mental hospital in Bielefeld, The Retreat still exists today. It is a 100-bed independent hospital and still has monthly animal visitors, plus a dedicated Pets Corner where patients can look after the hospital's own resident pets.

Animals at The Retreat today

Resident Quaker Bronwen Gray says that animals have been part of The Retreat since it was founded and that the current Pets Corner features guinea pigs, hamsters and a rabbit, cared for by patients, staff and volunteers.

> A painting dating from 1900 shows three dogs in the foreground, and in our own time we have had regular visits from a Pets as Therapy (PAT) dog. We now have three, and patients have responded very positively, making it clear they really value this contact.

One patient says,

> Working at Pets Corner has really helped my recovery. I hate animal cruelty and though I only clean them on a Sunday, it makes me happy that they are well looked after, and gives me a sense of pride. When I come back to the Unit I feel much calmer and more relaxed.

Bronwen adds that the latest animals to arrive have been regular visitors from a local animal sanctuary called Nuzzlets.

Once a month, people flock to the main hall where there is likely to be a goat, chickens, rabbits, and sometimes ducks and sheep. A field let out to a local farmer is home to half-a-dozen horses whose presence is very much appreciated. We also have a fantastic variety of wild animals in our grounds.

Another pioneer of animal therapy was the founder of modern nursing, Florence Nightingale. She was an animal-lover herself and is on record as having owned about 60 cats during her lifetime!

'Cats,' she once said, 'possess more sympathy and feeling than human beings.'

Her mother told the press that young Florence 'always had a passion for almost any kind of creature'. Even her interest in nursing was apparently awakened when she cared for an injured sheepdog when she was 17.

Florence Nightingale observed that having a pet to care for was effective in reducing anxiety in both children and psychiatric patients and wrote in her famous handbook *Notes on Nursing*, published in 1859, that being with animals could help patients to recover.

'A pet bird in a cage is sometimes the only pleasure of an invalid confined for years to the same room,' she said. 'A small pet is often an excellent companion for the sick, and for long, chronic cases especially.'

At around the time that Miss Nightingale was recommending animal therapy for her patients, a blind Swiss gentleman named Jakob Birrer was describing how he had trained his own dog to act as a guide. This wasn't the first known example of a dog being used in this way. There is a mural at Roman Herculaneum dating from the first century AD which shows a dog clearly leading a blind man, and a Viennese doctor in the early nineteenth century had also mentioned the idea. However, it wasn't until the devastation of the First World War that the idea of guide dogs really began to take shape. Many soldiers from all sides had been blinded in gas attacks, and a German doctor called Gerhard Stalling opened the first-ever training school for guide dogs in the German city of Oldenburg.

Hundreds of dogs were trained to be companions to blind veterans. An American lady called Dorothy Eustis took up the idea and introduced it to the United States. A blind American named Morris Frank was teamed up with the first 'seeing eye' dog, Buddy, in 1928.

Britain was not far behind. Two ladies from Cheshire, Muriel Crooke and Rosamund Bond, trained the UK's first four guide dogs from modest premises in a garage in Wallasey under the supervision of Mrs Eustis, and in October 1931 the dogs were matched up with their blind owners. Today, Guide Dogs for the Blind supports around 4,800 owners and their dogs and they have been followed by other 'assistance animals' from hearing dogs for the deaf to medical detection dogs (see Chapter 5).

It was also in the 1930s that the work of Sigmund Freud, the 'father of psychoanalysis', began to be widely known and appreciated. Less well known at the time was the fact that Freud had found out, almost by accident, how helpful his pet dog Jofi was to his patients. He had only become a dog-lover in later life when Jofi was given to him by his daughter Anna. The dog sat in on the doctor's therapy sessions and Freud discovered that his patients felt much more comfortable talking about their problems if the dog was there. Some of them even preferred to talk to Jofi, rather than the doctor! Freud noted that if the dog sat near the patient, the patient found it easier to relax, but if Jofi sat on the other side of the room, the patient seemed more tense and distressed. He was surprised to realize that Jofi seemed to sense this too. The dog's presence was an especially calming influence on child and teenage patients.

Although Freud made a note of this in his writings, the idea of using animals in therapy sessions wasn't really taken seriously for about another 30 years, until the idea was taken up by an American psychologist called Boris Levinson. Dr Levinson was working with a very withdrawn and disturbed little boy who found it difficult to communicate. He found that the lad opened up much more if the doctor's dog Jingles was present at their therapy sessions.

When Dr Levinson reported on this at medical and psychiatric conferences, he was laughed at to begin with. Once his fellow-professionals were made aware that Freud had noticed the same phenomenon and had mentioned it in his own writings, the idea of 'animal-assisted therapy' or AAT – a term coined by Dr Levinson in 1964 – slowly began to gain acceptance. By the early 1970s Dr Levinson found that 16 per cent of psychotherapists were using animals in their sessions. Pets were 'prescribed' for people with mental and emotional problems because they were found to improve social skills, ease anxiety, improve mood, make independent living easier and more pleasurable, boost confidence, reduce loneliness . . . and supply all the advantages that pet owners instinctively believe! Further research studies have also found that contact with animals benefits humans' physical health, as we shall see in the next chapter.

2

Pets and your physical health

Pets keep you healthy!

In 2004 there was an International Conference on Human/Animal Interactions in Glasgow. Bruce Headey from the University of Melbourne in Australia presented a paper based on a large research study on the relationship between pet ownership and health, involving more than 11,000 people. The main findings were that

- people who own pets continuously are the healthiest group, with significantly fewer visits to their GP than other people;
- people who have not had a pet before, but who later get one, are the second healthiest group;
- the least healthy group, those who visit their GP most often, are people who have never owned a pet!

When animal-assisted therapy began to be taken seriously by the medical profession back in the 1970s, researchers started looking at how, exactly, owning or being in contact with animals could improve people's physical health. Over the next 20 or 30 years, many research studies discovered that pets could offer much more than just a comforting presence. They could actually affect physical health – both in preventing illness in the first place, and in helping humans to recover from it afterwards.

A wealth of information from the 1980s onwards suggested that pet ownership – and other kinds of contact with animals – could affect

- the human stress response;
- blood pressure levels;
- cholesterol and tri-glyceride levels, which also have an impact on heart health;
- the speed at which people recovered from serious illnesses, including heart attacks;

- the strength of the human immune system and its ability to fight infection;
- even the number of times people went to their GP with minor ailments like coughs, colds and hay fever.

On a very basic level, this could be because people with animals in their lives tend to be more active, and we all know that exercise – with or without an animal companion – is good for us. Regular exercise for at least 30 minutes a day, three times a week, is the minimum recommended by doctors in order to reduce the risk of some of the most common killers, such as heart disease, stroke and some forms of cancer. Active people are also less likely to suffer from Type 2 diabetes and asthma. What better excuse to get out there and get walking than becoming a dog owner? Rain or shine, your canine friend is always ready for a walk. Playing games with him can elevate levels of the 'feel-good' hormones like serotonin and dopamine. A Canadian research study in 2006 found that dog owners were likely to walk for 300 minutes a week compared to 168 minutes for non-owners.

Walking the dog may be the most obvious, but it isn't the only way in which animals encourage people to exercise. As long ago as the 1870s, a French doctor was recommending horse-riding for those with disabilities, reporting that it helped with their balance and motor control. In our own time, the organization Riding for the Disabled has continued with the same work. They are currently helping some 28,000 people with all kinds of disabilities from cerebral palsy to muscular dystrophy. For people without disabilities, horse-riding can also help with physical fitness, as a study published by the British Horse Society in 2011 discovered. Their researchers, based at the University of Brighton and Plumpton College, found that

- most riders rode for 30 minutes or more, at least three times a week, which is the government's recommended minimum for exercise;
- the movement involved in riding and caring for a horse, including activities such as mucking out, could be classified as 'moderate exercise';
- the majority of the riders surveyed, some 90 per cent, were

women, and 37 per cent of those were aged 45 or more, which indicates that riding is a form of exercise which attracts this age group;

- the motion of trotting was particularly beneficial;
- quotes from the riders interviewed showed that those with health problems such as rheumatoid arthritis, multiple sclerosis, ME (sometimes known as Chronic Fatigue Syndrome), back pain and dislocated shoulders found that riding was extremely therapeutic. Even riders with painful knees and limited mobility, who were normally crutch or wheelchair users, found riding benefited their physical health.

As long ago as the 1980s, doctors were finding that contact with animals could reduce stress in human beings. Stress symptoms such as raised blood pressure are reduced, for example, when patients in dentists' waiting rooms are able to watch a tank of tropical fish. Stroking a dog, or even having a dog in the same room, can lead to the same response and increase the levels of the hormone oxytocin. Sometimes known as the 'cuddle hormone', oxytocin plays an important role in the formation of emotional bonds between people, and also between people and animals. When dogs and humans gaze into one another's eyes, oxytocin levels rise in both of them! Later research studies have found that even watching videos featuring animals can lower the stress response. In the 1990s, Australian researchers found that even short interactions, lasting from 5 to 25 minutes, between people and animals led to physical benefits like the slowing-down of heart rates and a reduction in stress hormones. Longer interactions, for instance actually owning a pet, were found to help people live longer and recover faster after serious illness such as a heart attack. Older pet owners also make fewer visits to their doctors than people who don't have pets.

Since stress seems to be such a modern epidemic, with everyone from exam candidates to overworked commuters complaining of being stressed-out, it's worth having a look at the human stress response and how contact with animals can help us to counteract it.

What happens to your body when you're stressed?

The human body is designed to respond to stress in a variety of ways. They are all very real and they are physical as well as psychological. The 'fight-or-flight response', as it's known, is a survival mechanism which is hard-wired in all of us. Primitive man, faced with a charging mammoth or a sabre-toothed tiger, responded in the same way as a frustrated motorist stuck in a traffic jam or a mother trying to cope with several fractious children. Primitive man had the choice of hitting the creature with his club or running for it, with a surge of the same hormones as his modern counterpart.

When you are stressed your heart rate increases and your blood pressure rises. You breathe more quickly, you sweat more, your digestion and other unnecessary systems temporarily 'shut down' to divert your body's energy to fighting – or fleeing.

How does this happen? Your brain's 'command centre', the hypothalamus, sends signals to the pituitary gland, stimulating it to produce something called ACTH or adrenocorticotropic hormone. This, in its turn, stimulates your adrenal glands to produce one of the main stress hormones, cortisol, whose function is to enable your body to maintain its supply of blood sugars, needed to power your muscles. At the same time your adrenal medulla secretes the other stress hormone, adrenaline, which is responsible for 'switching off' your digestion, the rise in blood pressure and the increase in sweating.

Stress, of course, is not all bad. If you genuinely are in danger it enables you to escape, and a life without any stress at all would be really dull! However, repeated stress can contribute to continually raised blood pressure, leading to stroke illness and to furred-up arteries, which are a risk factor for heart attacks. Too many adrenaline surges can damage blood vessels and arteries, too many cortisol surges can increase appetite and lead to obesity with all its well-known health risks. It follows that anything that can balance your fight-or-flight response with its opposite, and more beneficial, rest-and-recovery response, will improve your health.

A therapy dog was even introduced to passengers at San Jose International Airport to reassure them after the trauma of the attacks on the World Trade Center in 2001 and around 30 US airports now include friendly, trained dogs to soothe and calm nervous or stressed passengers. Even more recently, in 2012 the British Psychological Society reported that job satisfaction is said to go up in workplaces where dogs are allowed. Professor Randolph Barker, of the School of Business Studies at Virginia Commonwealth University, said that 'Pet presence may serve as a low-cost, wellness intervention readily available to many organizations.'

It has also been suggested that having pets in the office could benefit workers, although a study by the Purina pet food company in 2015 found that 82 per cent of companies in Britain did not allow this. They also discovered that half of dog owners would like to bring their pooch to work with them. In 1996 'Take your dog to work day' was introduced in Britain, and the presence of friendly dogs was said to reduce workers' stress levels, increase job satisfaction, help team co-operation and boost morale! With the increasing concern about obesity levels, plus the fact that many office jobs involve sitting in front of a screen for as much as seven hours a day, having to get up and walk your dog in your lunch break would seem to benefit everyone – and, according to a study quoted in the *International Journal of Workplace Health Management*, pets in the office have a calming effect and can actually increase productivity.

As well as helping to reduce the stress symptoms which may lead to heart attacks, the presence of animals can also help patients recover from them. Research studies as long ago as 1980 found that dog owners were more than eight times as likely to be alive a year after their heart attack than those who did not have a pet. And it isn't just dogs: in 2008 another study found that cat owners had a 30 per cent lower risk of death from a heart attack than non-owners.

Therapy animals can also be helpful in the rehabilitation of stroke patients. Sallie Bolland is the founder of an organization called Stroke Rehab Dogs, based in Enfield, north London. She says,

> I had heard of Pets as Therapy back in 2004, when a PAT dog visited my young nephew in hospital. I wondered if dogs could be used to help elderly people, including stroke patients, and got in touch with the Society for Companion Animal Studies to do some research, eventually launching my own project.

Therapy has to be fun and beneficial for the patient, the dog and the volunteer who owns the dog. Our dogs are assessed for suitability, like all therapy animals. They have to like being with people, being fussed and groomed. I have a team of eight at the moment. All of them have different skills which help us to meet the goals of individual patients.

For example, we have a dog who responds to signs and whistles and he works with a patient with aphasia (communication difficulties). Just the fact that a living creature responded to him was such a boost to his recovery and self-confidence. Someone who no longer had awareness of one side of his body, or who has lost the use of one hand, might be encouraged to use their stronger hand to lift the weaker one, and then use the weak hand to brush and groom the dog. Other patients have body image problems and may not recognize the parts of the body. They learn to match a picture of the dog's paw to the real-life paw and then touch it.

This kind of therapy isn't for everyone, but if a patient has an affinity with dogs it can make a real difference. It is relaxed and non-threatening, it enables them to stand for longer and to exercise for longer. They might have felt silly or embarrassed trying to speak but having a dog there reduces their tension and anxiety and introduces humour to their rehab programme. There are so many advantages to working with therapy animals!

Chronic health conditions for which there doesn't seem to be any instant cure or 'quick fix' have also been shown to benefit from animal-assisted therapy. One example is fibromyalgia, a long-term condition which can cause pain all over the body as well as symptoms such as muscle stiffness, difficulty sleeping, headaches and memory problems. The calming effect of a friendly dog has been tested by the National Fibromyalgia and Chronic Pain Association in the USA. Patients due for hospital appointments could choose to sit in a traditional waiting room with a TV and magazines, or another with a friendly and well-trained dog. Those who spent time with the dog experienced a 'significant reduction' in pain, anxiety and distress, with 34 per cent reporting less pain and more than 60 per cent reporting feeling calmer and more cheerful. Those in the other waiting room reported no difference.

There is a possibility, too, that contact with animals could benefit the human immune system. It's known that the incidence of allergic disease and conditions such as eczema has risen over the last 30 or 40 years, and the reason for this rise is not yet known. One possibility is what is known as the 'Hygiene Hypothesis', which states that because we are so much cleaner and so much more germ-aware than previous generations, our bodies don't get a chance to build up any immunity. It is known that people who grow up on farms – obviously having more-than-average contact with animals – and who are exposed to animal dander (a mixture of hair or fur and saliva) are less likely to develop allergies. James E. Gern, a paediatrician at the University of Wisconsin, published some research in the *Journal of Allergy and Clinical Immunology* which showed that babies brought up with dogs showed fewer signs of pet allergies or eczema, and that they also had fewer colds and ear infections in their first year of life than babies in pet-free homes.

3

Pets and mental health

You don't have to look very far to find examples of animals helping to improve their owners' mental, psychological and emotional health. One of the most famous, in recent years, is Street Cat Bob, the stray ginger cat who appeared in the stairwell of recovering addict James Bowen's supported housing flat in north London in 2007. James, who had had a difficult upbringing and had spent some time sleeping rough on the streets of London, took in the injured stray, fed him, got him medical treatment – and the two have been together ever since.

James had earned a precarious living for himself and Bob as a busker and *Big Issue* vendor when they came to the attention of a literary agent. Their story, told by James in the book *A Street Cat Named Bob*, topped the British best-seller list, has now sold more than five million copies worldwide, has been translated into more than 35 languages, and has been made into a film.

'Bob has totally changed my life. I owe it all to him,' James says. 'He's my best mate and the one who has guided me to a different – and better – way of life.'

In late 2014 a touching story appeared on the national TV news about Sheila Marsh, 77, a terminally ill cancer patient being cared for at the Royal Albert Edward Infirmary in Wigan. Nurses arranged for her favourite horse, Bronwen, to be brought to the hospital car park and wheeled Sheila's bed down there so that she and Bronwen could see each other for one last time.

Every other year the charity Cats Protection runs the 'National Cat Awards' featuring similar heart-warming stories about the impact adopting and caring for a rescue cat has on the lives of all kinds of people – especially those who would otherwise be struggling. Contenders for the most recent 'Caring Cat' section included Elias, a Turkish Van who is the mainstay and support for an Army veteran who suffers from post-traumatic stress disorder after serving in Northern Ireland. There was also ginger Clementine, who helped a couple through the husband's five-month recovery after a serious accident and the wife's severe depression, and a tortoiseshell named Maci who is credited with boosting an unhappy, bullied teenager's confidence sufficiently to enable her to return to college and later find a job.

In 2011, a joint research project between Cats Protection and the Mental Health Foundation looked at more than 600 people with mental health problems, some with cats, some without. The project found that 87 per cent thought their cat had a positive impact on their well-being, while 76 per cent said their cat helped them cope better with everyday life. Half said that 'companionship' was the most important quality their cat offered them, and a third said that stroking the cat was most helpful and calming.

Dogs are also more than just loving companions to people with depression, anxiety and other mental health issues. The campaigning organization Dogs for Depression is trying to raise awareness of the emotional support dogs can give, and hoping that the UK will follow the USA in providing psychological assistance dogs to those who can benefit from them, in the same way as Guide Dogs for the Blind and Canine Partners for disabled people (see Chapter 5). They make the point that dogs are pack animals and tend to bond with their 'pack' or family. They say that the advantages of dog ownership include:

- Dogs are a calming presence and owners are drawn to patting and stroking them.
- The touch of a dog's fur is soothing.
- Dogs offer troubled people unconditional love. They have no agenda of their own; they don't care if you are old or young, plain or beautiful – you are simply *theirs*.
- Dogs don't try to give advice or get angry when you don't take it. They just love you.
- Being loved by your dog can raise your self-esteem.
- Being a dog owner is excellent for reducing the feelings of isolation experienced by many lonely people. Dog owners – and walkers – always meet others!
- Attending training classes or dog shows introduces you to other humans as well as other dogs.

- Dogs respond instinctively to your body language or tone of voice, rather than your actual words, which can be useful for those who have trouble expressing themselves.
- Dogs can make you laugh!

In 2014 the book *My Dog, My Friend* by mental health researcher Jacki Gordon was published, with all royalties going to the Samaritans, the charity which offers a 24/7 listening ear to anyone in trouble or despair. Samaritans trustee Professor Stephen Platt said that there is a great deal of evidence that dogs benefit human health and well-being.

We believe that *My Dog, My Friend* will increase awareness about the important role that animals, and dogs in particular, can play in helping people who are struggling to cope. What is striking from the contributors in this book is the many different ways in which dogs support us in our daily lives.

Jacki says,

Because of my background working in mental health, I was aware how much dogs could help people with conditions such as depression. When I got my own dog I was struck by the positive impact she had on my life. I went out more, I met more people, I was never alone and she made me laugh.

When I decided to write the book I took a look at the body of evidence about how much dog ownership can help – it's not just anecdotal. The responses I got from those I interviewed were all very different and varied from the laugh-out-loud funny to the incredibly moving. A man with multiple sclerosis who was twinned with a Canine Partner said she had had a transformative effect on his well-being and given him a reason to live. Someone with borderline personality disorder said her dog kept her safe. Later, at a book festival, I was approached by a woman with a black Labrador who told me she had had depression for decades, as well as agoraphobia and an alcohol problem – until a friend had dropped a puppy into her arms and she had fallen in love. From that day onwards she had opened her curtains, gone out for walks and given up drinking because she knew she wouldn't be able to look after her dog if she was in an alcoholic stupor.

I'm not saying that everyone with mental illness should get a dog. You have to be in the right place. But dogs can and do have a positive impact on mental health.

Loneliness and lack of self-esteem are among the most obvious conditions which can be alleviated by living with an animal friend. You are never alone with a dog or cat – as Jacki says, walking the dog brings you into contact with other people and makes it infinitely easier to strike up a conversation with strangers. Local cat owners often get to know one another too, as it is common for cats to wander into their neighbours' gardens (and houses!) and for neighbours to exchange cat-sitting duties during holiday times. Having the responsibility for a pet can increase your sense of your own value and importance. Caring for an animal reminds you that however low you might feel, you are capable. When you're tempted to stay in bed and pull the covers over your head, you *have* to get up and feed the cat or walk the dog. That everyday routine with a creature who needs you can be extremely soothing.

People with mental health issues can benefit from contact with all kinds of animals, not just domestic pets. In the UK there are about 230 'care farms', an idea which was pioneered in the Netherlands. These may be large commercial farms, community farms or smallholdings. Most are regular farms where the farmers are interested in farming holistically, but some are specifically set up to be care farms. What they offer is a supervised programme of farming-related activities suitable for vulnerable people, most of who are referred by Social Services. Some are learning disabled, some are autistic, some have a history of drug abuse, others may be on probation.

Clinks Care Farm

Clinks Care Farm in Suffolk is a mixed farm with pigs, sheep, chickens and goats as well as crops. They employ 'farm helpers' who can choose what they want to do and who are involved in all the activities. Some of the helpers have learning difficulties or brain injuries, some are on the autistic spectrum or have diagnoses of bipolar or schizophrenia. Clinks also works through an innovative scheme called 'Farming on Prescription' by which local GPs or the

WellBeing service can refer patients who have conditions such as depression and anxiety, as an alternative to medication.

The animal teams, made up of staff, volunteers and helpers, are involved with all the work of the farm, so the helpers might be collecting and grading eggs from 150 chickens, feeding and watering the pigs or weaning the piglets by separating them from the sow and separating males from females, worming the sheep and checking them for fly strike, or reporting back if they have any concerns about the animals' welfare, such as lameness, injury or unusual behaviour.

'Each person who comes here will take something different away from the experience,' says their spokeswoman.

> We see an increase in their confidence and self-esteem when they realize that they have learned new skills and become more independent. They learn to be patient and calm and do things slowly. Animals are non-judgemental, unlike some people. We had a man here who hadn't worked for 12 years because of depression. When he left us he got a job straight away. Another, who had social anxiety, worked with our pigs and is now managing a unit at a pig farm. Having to care for animals gives structure to the day – however you feel, you have to get up and feed and water them!

Equine-assisted therapy

Winston Churchill once said, 'There is something about the outside of a horse that is good for the inside of a man.' We saw in the previous chapter how therapy involving horses can improve people's physical health, but 'equine-assisted therapy' in various forms is increasingly being used to help with mental health as well. Attention Deficit Disorder, post-traumatic stress, anxiety, autism, depression, brain injury, addictions and many other conditions can sometimes be improved by this kind of therapy.

Equine-assisted therapy is actually said to date back to the Ancient Greeks! It doesn't always involve riding, although it may do. Sometimes the patients don't even touch the horse at first; sometimes they learn to groom and care for it and build up a relationship that way. There are many independent organizations working with horses and people, for example Devon-based Sirona Therapeutic Horsemanship and LEAP in Gloucestershire. One of the teachers and psychotherapists at Sirona simply says, 'Horses can teach humans so much about trust, love and healing.'

Equine-assisted therapy can be used by physio-, occupational and speech and language therapists as part of a individually designed programme, and usually involves a horse or horses, therapists and a horse expert. It can help both individuals and groups to

- discover more about themselves and develop new and healthier ways of thinking;
- interact and form a relationship with the horse by leading it without a bridle or rope;
- think creatively about how to do this;
- talk to the therapist about the experience and how it made them feel – which can benefit patients who have had trouble expressing themselves.

Why is this form of animal therapy so successful? Those who use it say that there can be a deep and profound connection between humans and horses. It seems that neuroscience has recently discovered similarities between the 'emotional' brains of horses and people, so perhaps Sir Winston got it right! Part of the reason might be that horses are large and powerful animals which can seem intimidating at first. Getting a horse to trust you and follow your instructions can be liberating and empowering in itself and increase a patient's confidence and self-esteem, so that he or she is better able to form relationships with people. Horses are herd animals who *want* to form bonds and have fun with other creatures – including humans. They read and respond to a person's body language – whether that person is fearful and defensive, or calm and confident.

Even the most severely mentally ill people can often benefit from animal-assisted therapy. The State Hospital in Lanarkshire, Scotland's high-security mental hospital, has been using it as part of a holistic approach to treating their patients for some time.

These are very sick people. The majority have been diagnosed with schizophrenia, about a quarter have another diagnosis and some have multiple problems. On average, patients spend seven years in the hospital, with some having to stay much longer.

On-site animals include rabbits, guinea pigs, kune kune pigs, goats and hens. Patients are encouraged to handle, feed and care for the animals, and many find bonding with other creatures much easier than getting people to know and trust them. At one point a pigeon loft was set up for patients in the learning disability ward. Being able to handle the birds gently and rear youngsters gave the patients a sense of achievement and well-being. The animals are seen as important sources of support and provide non-judgemental companionship to people whose backgrounds have often been extremely troubled.

Learning about different creatures and their care needs means that staff see patients develop better concentration, increased ability to process information, and changing attitudes. Patients who were previously distant and hostile show a caring side towards the animals, and are sometimes able to talk about pets they have lost. Those who were aggressive seem calmer when they are with the animals. A woman who had regularly attacked staff and other patients and damaged her room was gentle and caring with the Animal Therapy Centre's guinea pigs, and was pleasant to both staff and other patients after she had spent time with the animals.

More than 70 per cent of those in prisons in the UK have two or more mental health disorders – and prisoners, too, can benefit from contact with animals. In fact, the Ministry of Justice sometimes allows those serving life sentences to keep a pet bird. In the autumn of 2014, two rescue Labradors and a number of ex-battery hens were introduced into Hydebank Wood Young Offenders Centre and Prison in Belfast. The idea of the project was to help troubled prisoners and promote resilience and positive health. The Northern Ireland Prison Service's Director General, Sue McAlister, explained:

> While there is a well-known and accepted benefit to pet owner-ship, the therapeutic benefits are less well known. Our re-homed Labradors and two of our dog handlers have taught prisoners how to look after the dogs, including obedience training, exercising and agility work. Looking after the dogs has had a very positive effect on prisoners.
>
> Managing and caring for the hens has also had therapeutic ben-efits, as well as providing fresh, free-range eggs! We have found a positive change in the behaviours of the women involved, which

is not only good for their health and well-being, but also for our staff and the wider community.

Safe touch

The concept of 'safe touch' is a central one in animal-assisted therapy for survivors of trauma, whether in the form of post-traumatic stress disorder or for those recovering from, for example, childhood sexual abuse or domestic violence.

Devon-based counsellor and psychotherapist Sarah Urwin has years of experience of working with animals and says that her clients have benefited.

'Animal-assisted therapy is definitely written about more these days,' she says,

> even though the medical establishment is still waiting for more hard, empirical research evidence. It is easy enough to measure someone's physiological responses – we can see blood pressure going down – but much harder to evaluate 'softer' skills such as resilience or increased self-esteem! I have had animals all my life and they have helped to keep me sane. In 2002 I was working in a residential addiction unit. I took my dog to work and noticed how the clients responded to him. People are naturally drawn to animals whether they are dogs, horses or chickens. Animals are non-judgemental and non-critical. Touch is a central tenet of AAT, irrespective of the kind of animal. There is research evidence that stroking brings down the heart rate, but it's more than that. Working with people who have been traumatized I am aware that many have only ever experienced unsafe touch, either in terms of violence or sexual abuse. When they have experienced 'safe touch' through stroking or patting an animal, they can slowly learn what touch really means. They learn to trust because they know the animal is not going to hurt them, and eventually they can transfer that trust to their human relationships.
>
> Some people I work with have suffered horrendous abuse. I have worked with women living in refuges who have never experienced any real intimacy in any of their relationships. I carefully match the person I'm working with to the animals here. As an example, some women will respond to small creatures such as guinea pigs which will sit on their laps, cuddle in, and just emit

one of their 37 different types of squeak! That may be a perfect situation for a woman who couldn't possibly stand up and stroke a large animal like a horse.

The 'matching' process is important. Some autistic children may be frightened of dogs, for example, though not all are. Other clients are happy to tell their secrets to a friendly animal – a dog or a horse – before they tell their human therapist. AAT is a two-way communication process, with animals seeming happy to see the client, showing them affection, 'choosing' to be with them, in a way that the abusive human beings in their lives may never have done.

4

Pets and older people

The everyday benefits of pet ownership are pretty much the same for older people as they are for everyone else. Walking the dog gives you a reason to exercise, brings you into contact with other people, and improves your physical and mental health, whether you are 17 or 70! However, it is also true that there are particular benefits to older people, which have been outlined by organizations like the National Careline and the Society for Companion Animal Studies. They say that the main advantages of having a pet in later life are

- companionship – especially for those who live alone, as two million over-75s do;
- giving structure to the day, especially post-retirement when, unless plans have been made to acquire new interests, life can suddenly change from being very busy to extremely empty;
- reminders to those older folk who are frail and forgetful to take care of their pet – having to buy and prepare food for the cat or dog means that they are less likely to neglect their own meals, and wanting to keep the animal warm can encourage them to put the heating on;
- an increase in activity and stimulation;
- less demand on health and social care services.

Isolation can be a particular problem for older people. According to a 2015 survey by Age UK, around 2.9 million older people in the UK feel that they have no-one to turn to. Of these, 39 per cent say they are lonely and 20 per cent feel they have been forgotten. As many as one in ten, apparently, are in touch with family, friends or neighbours less often than once a month. This says a lot about how twenty-first-century Britain looks after its older folk – but it also underlines how important the companionship of a dog or cat or other pet can be to them.

While older people are fit and well and living in their own homes, pet ownership is straightforward enough. However, problems can arise when they become frail and unable to live alone any longer. Then a move to residential care, sheltered housing or a care or nursing home has to be considered. This is something that concerns many old people. Worry about their pet is one reason why they may resist a necessary move to more suitable accommodation. It's something that animal charities are very aware of and are taking steps to help with, although at the moment most of them seem to focus on schemes which guarantee that an animal will be re-homed if the owner dies. The Blue Cross has its 'Pets into Care' scheme; the Dogs Trust offers a 'Canine Care Card'; Cats Protection has a 'Cat Guardians' service.

Pet Promise

Wood Green: The Animals Charity has a free scheme called 'Pet Promise' in which, once your animals are registered with them, they guarantee that they will take them in, care for them and re-home them if you are ill or go into residential care, as well as taking them on if you pass away.

When you register – and you can register as many pets as you want – you will be asked for their details and then sent a 'Care Card' with your pet's enrolment number, which you can carry with you at all times. You are also sent collar tags for your pet, stickers to leave in a prominent place in your home, and information about adding your wishes to your will.

All animal welfare charities are sympathetic to owners who have legitimate reasons, such as old age and infirmity, for giving up their pets. The National Animal Welfare Trust has a retirement centre for older animals near Hungerford in Berkshire. They have a long waiting list but are able to re-home some of their elderly pets ('Not everyone wants a puppy!' they say). Those who stay with them live in homely, heated accommodation with sofas and TVs as well as outdoor runs for exercise.

The Cinnamon Trust

One particular charity, the Cinnamon Trust, based in Cornwall, was actually set up to help the elderly and terminally ill and their pets. Their 15,000-plus volunteers all over the country will step in when needed and

- walk dogs for housebound older folk;
- foster pets on a short-term basis if an elderly owner has to go into hospital;
- buy the cat or dog food, clean out the birdcage or do whatever is required.

If the old person is worried about what will happen to her animal after she has passed away, she can arrange with the Trust to take care of it, either in the two sanctuaries they run themselves, or by re-homing the animal, often to an owner who has lost his own much-loved companion.

People and Pets Advocates is another charity which is intended to provide shared care for pets in difficult times. Their volunteers provide fostering and/or respite care while an owner is in hospital, for example.

The issue of pets in sheltered housing, care and nursing homes is one which, not surprisingly, concerns the Society for Companion Animal Studies (SCAS) as well. In 2007 they produced a 'Report on Pets in Residential Care' which, in its turn, was a follow-up to a similar study from the Joseph Rowntree Foundation in the 1990s. The earlier study had discovered that many older people were made to give up their pets when they went into care, and by 2007 very little had changed.

The SCAS study found that

- approximately 2.75 million elderly people needing care were pet owners;
- 60 per cent of care facilities required them to give up their pets and many pets had to be put to sleep for this reason;
- in 39 per cent of care homes, staff noticed that patients were distressed at the idea of parting with their pets;
- many homes which do allow pets only allow one per resident – which means old people may be faced with an impossible choice;

- care homes were concerned about their liability for accidents caused by pets, or pet-acquired illnesses, though there was little evidence of this ever happening;
- only 30 per cent of care homes had an official policy on pets.

However, there are signs that things are changing. There is now a focus on what is known as 'person-centred care', which means that older people in residential care can expect to be treated as individuals, with lives of value and achievement, rather than just simply 'cases'. A care home is just that – a *home* – where residents should not have to give up all choice or control over their own lives. According to the charity Independent Age, care home residents should be able to please themselves how they live their lives, providing they are safe and respect others' rights too. The emphasis should be on what residents *can* do, rather than what they cannot – and if they wish, this should of course include having a pet. A much-loved dog, cat or budgie may be a cherished link to their previous life, perhaps reminding them of a partner who has died, their family, their younger days and their memories. Losing a pet – especially if the 'loss' is forced on them – can lead to grief and depression, which helps nobody.

The Cinnamon Trust (see p. 27) produces a book called *Pet Friendly Care Homes* and has made awards to the 'Pet Friendly Care Home of the Year'. Annie Sinnott, the owner of the Old Vicarage in Dorset, the winner of this award in 2013, said that as far as they were concerned, residents' pets were family and she would never think of separating them. She feels that having pets helps to calm and reassure all the residents, not just the owners themselves. Many of the activities organized by this particular home involve animals in one way or another, from summer visits to local smallholdings to reindeer appearing with Santa at Christmas!

'We have had animals at the Old Vicarage for 30 years and have only had good experiences,' Annie adds.

> We have never had animals that have clashed in any way. We've had cats who have changed rooms and carers many times, but always stay with us. Many have been rescue pets and seem pleased to have found a warm home! There are many tears from the staff when they have to leave us as the majority of the staff

are animal-lovers. There are smiles from the residents as having cats on their laps can reduce blood pressure and stress levels. We currently have four cats and four dogs around. I feel that just as care home residents should have their own furniture and photos, they should have their pets too!

There do seem to be moves among some care providers to allow older people to keep their pets – or to provide 'community pets' as companions for their residents. Sunrise, one of the major care providers, says that pets make residents feel good, can help to ease the pain caused by arthritis or migraine, and increase brain activity. They say that taking care of an animal can give older people a sense of purpose, keep them active and benefit their physical health too, and that many of the Sunrise communities have a resident cat or dog.

Another major care provider, Anchor, now says that it has a pet-friendly policy covering all its retirement housing and care homes. Residents are allowed to have pets as long as they are properly looked after and don't cause any problems for the other residents. Courtesy and common-sense suggest that cats and dogs should be kept away from neighbours who have allergies, or who really dislike or are afraid of them.

The SCAS say that the true risk of animals transmitting diseases to frail old people does need to be discussed, but that residents are far more likely to catch something from their human visitors than from animals! There *are* infections, called 'zoonoses', which can be passed from animals to people, but in normal circumstances this route of infection is rare, especially when basic hygiene precautions are taken, for example making sure that

- all the animals involved are healthy, have been treated for worms and fleas, and have regular check-ups from a vet;
- those cleaning up after the animals use poo bags and rubber gloves;
- everyone washes their hands with soap and hot water after contact with the animals, and especially before preparing or eating food.

In 2013 the SCAS produced a 'Pet-Friendly Care Kit' intended for housing providers, to help them create a safe care environment where residents can benefit from contact with animals. They say that, in the minority of care facilities where animals are present either as personal pets or visitors, both staff and residents report that

- residents feel happier and more at home;
- the animals become an important part of the home's daily life;
- 99 per cent of the problems caused are minor and easily resolved; and
- the extra work for the staff is minimal.

Pets as Therapy

The charity Pets as Therapy (PAT) was founded in the 1980s to bring the benefit of contact with friendly animals to people who needed it. Nowadays, around 4,500 dogs and 180 cats visit around 130,000 people every week. Not all are elderly, but PAT animals are popular visitors in hospitals, hospices and care homes. Even the most withdrawn patients often respond and open up when their PAT visitor is around. Many associate companion animals with home comforts and are reminded of pets they have owned in the past.

PAT dogs and cats are owned by volunteers and carefully assessed before they are awarded their name tag and PAT hi-vis jacket! Dogs need to be able to:

- walk on a lead without pulling or jumping up;
- be under their owner's control at all times;
- be happy to be stroked, patted and handled by strangers (sometimes vigorously!);
- take a food treat without snatching;
- be calm, clean and well groomed;
- cope with unfamiliar noises and equipment – wheelchairs, for example.

Cats need to:

- be able to relax and feel happy in unfamiliar surroundings;
- be ready to explore and approach humans without seeming frightened or running away to hide;

- be prepared to be held and stroked by strangers;
- be clean, well groomed, fit and healthy.

Pets and dementia

Animal therapy is increasingly being used to help patients with dementia. As the population ages, this distressing condition is becoming more and more common. As yet there is no cure and treatment is mostly a matter of making sure people with Alzheimer's – the most common form – and other dementias, plus their carers, are still able to enjoy their lives as far as possible. Animals can be part of that.

There is considerable anecdotal evidence and also scientific research into the benefits animal therapy offers patients with dementia. Contact with a friendly animal allows them to stroke or hug, bed-bound patients get the comfort of a cat or dog curling up beside them and it has even been known for dogs to gently lead a patient who wanders back to his or her room (we shall be looking at 'dementia dogs' in more detail in the next chapter).

The US journal *Annals of Longterm Care* reported in 2014 that animal therapy could delay the progression of some dementia symptoms such as aggression and agitation. When the researchers compared various forms of therapy, from bringing in stuffed toys and watching puppy videos to meeting a real dog, they found that the real animal got the best response, even helping non-verbal dementia patients to speak.

Researchers in Texas found that contact with animals could

- reduce agitation, which is common in people with Alzheimer's;
- increase physical activity – patients who had previously been quite passive were happy to walk, groom or throw a toy for a visiting dog;
- improve appetite – surprisingly, dementia patients, many of whom can forget to eat, actually ate more if a dog was in the room with them!

Like all therapy animals, those visiting people with dementia need the right calm temperament, as patients with these conditions can be unpredictable. They may be feeling bored or frustrated as they don't understand what is happening, where they are or what is expected of them. This can lead to challenging behaviour, aggression or what is known as 'sundowning', which refers to restlessness in the late afternoon or early evening. These symptoms can be alleviated by contact with a friendly animal.

Therapaws

The Mayhew Animal Home in north-west London has a special 'Therapaws' programme in which specially trained volunteers take their dogs to visit older people in care homes, 80 per cent of whom have some form of dementia, on a regular basis.

'We have a waiting list of care homes which are interested,' says Project Manager Luke Berman.

> Our volunteers take their own dogs, who have a half-hour temperamental assessment by a behaviourist to make sure they will be happy being stroked and touched all over by a stranger. They need to be calm, comfortable in busy environments, and under their owner's control at all times. I always go to the home first and the staff are excited by the idea because they know what a great thing it can be for residents. Often, on our visits, the staff want to meet the dogs too! Sometimes there are staff who come from parts of the world where dogs are not seen as pets so we are breaking down stereotypes.

> We see an immediate reaction from care home residents. When our volunteers arrive with the dog they 'wake up' straight away. They might call the dog, and even those without speech will gesture to bring the dog over. We know from the feedback we get that residents look forward to the day when the dog visits. They will wait by the windows and come into the lounge instead of staying in their rooms – though we do take the dogs to visit residents who are bed-bound too. Often, patting the dog will bring back memories of their own pets – sometimes from so long ago that even their families didn't know about them! We rely on staff to tell us if anyone has an allergy or is afraid of dogs, but there are very, very few people who don't benefit from our visits.

It is not only visiting cats and dogs which can improve the lives of older people in care facilities. Colin 'Geordie' Sutherland from

Berkshire rescues birds of prey and takes them to care homes all over the country, offering a personal, interactive experience to the residents with specially trained birds. His organization, Wings of Freedom, has introduced a barn owl called Rocky and a kestrel named Doris to local older folk with health problems including depression and dementia.

'I started doing this when I was a young lad, with my grandfather, who was years ahead of his time,' he says. 'I don't really know why it works, but it does!'

Henpower

Henpower, a project which began in the north-east of England in 2011 and is now being extended to other areas, introduced chickens into care homes after a gentleman who attended a Gateshead assessment centre told the staff he missed his friends Betty, Doreen, Pat and Pam. These 'ladies' turned out to be chickens! Funds were raised for a second-hand henhouse and six birds. The staff soon realized that elderly people, including those with dementia, benefit from having chickens to care for. Henpower isn't just about petting the creatures; they have to be looked after as well.

CEO Douglas Hunter says,

> This is different from other pet therapies because it involves a sense of shared responsibility. Residents may feed the hens, clean them or collect the eggs, and they are interacting with other residents and staff as well as the hens. The scheme also gives visiting family members something to talk about, and is a positive distraction for people with dementia, reducing any anxiety. We have seen positive results everywhere and staff agree that keeping chickens improves patients' quality of life.

A study by Northumbria University in 2012–13 found that the project improved the health and well-being of the old people, reduced depression and loneliness and meant that there was less need for anti-psychotic medication.

Our Special Friends

This is a Suffolk-based charity set up in 2014 by a vet, Belinda Johnston, who has a particular interest in bereavement issues for both people and animals.

'We need to look after humans and animals together,' she explains.

> There is so much information now about the importance of the human–animal bond and the fact that it is a special and meaningful relationship for both. We work with elderly and other vulnerable people, many of whom are terrified that their animals will be taken away. The difference between us and other organizations is that we are spanning the divide between human- and animal-focused help. We collaborate with other social and healthcare professionals to benefit humans, and with other animal welfare groups to benefit the animals. We work hard to keep people and their pets together if possible, to support them through bereavement, and to source companion animals, or visitors with animals, for those who have lost a pet or who can no longer keep one.
>
> As examples, one of our volunteers and her dog paid regular visits to a 93-year-old lady with advanced dementia and her carer. The carer told us that the visits 'brought her to life'! Also, through our involvement, domestic help was arranged for them which benefited both the lady and her carer. Another volunteer walked the dog of a lady who was no longer able to, having been diagnosed with a terminal illness, and also arranged for her family to take the dog to visit her in a hospice, where she was able to discuss her wishes about what would happen to her pet after she had died.
>
> We work with vulnerable people of any age, and with any kind of animal, locally at the moment but we hope to spread the word around the country!

5

Assistance animals

We have seen in previous chapters how the presence of a friendly animal can help people in all kinds of situations and with all kinds of difficulties, ranging from prisoners to frail old people in care and nursing homes. However, animals can offer more than just companionship, valuable though that is. Dogs in particular can also transform lives by being trained to perform tasks that their owners can't do, detect illnesses and medical crises before they happen, and generally act as the eyes, ears and limbs of people with disabilities. Animals' skills in these areas are being recognized more and more.

We saw in Chapter 1 how guide dogs for the blind were among the earliest examples of these 'assistance animals' and their work continues today in many parts of the world. Labrador retrievers Salty and Roselle were two guide dogs working with their owners at the World Trade Center in New York on September 11, 2001. Salty led his owner, Omar Rivera, down from the 71st floor to safety. Roselle led her owner, Michael Hingson, and 30 other people down to safety from the 78th floor. The two dogs were jointly awarded the PDSA's Dickin Medal for their courage and devotion.

In recent years guide dogs have been joined by others – hearing dogs for deaf people, support dogs for wheelchair users and those with epilepsy, Canine Partners trained to help people with even the most complex disabilities, medical detection dogs trained to 'sniff out' cancers or alert their diabetic owners to an approaching diabetic coma. Alzheimer Scotland is pioneering the use of 'dementia dogs' to help people with dementia manage their lives, and in some countries, such as the USA, there are projects using dogs to help people with psychological problems and war veterans with conditions such as post-traumatic stress.

The differences between therapy pets and assistance animals are sometimes slightly blurred, but generally 'assistance animals' are actually trained to help their owners with particular activities of daily living, for instance by alerting them to the ringing of the telephone or doorbell, reminding them that it is time to take their medication, or helping them to dress and undress – even collecting money from an ATM! One important difference between a therapy pet and an assistance animal is that the latter will have the right to accompany its owner into public places where animals are not generally allowed, for example shops, restaurants or on public transport.

Some organizations, for example Guide Dogs for the Blind, and Dogs for Good (formerly Dogs for the Disabled), breed and train their own animals, often Labradors, Golden Retrievers, Cocker Spaniels and similar breeds. Others will help clients to train their own dog to be an assistance animal providing its temperament is right for the job. Shrewsbury-based Dog A.I.D. (Assistance in Disability) does exactly that, providing (human) trainers to work with clients and their own dogs, which can be any breed up to 5 years old but must be assessed as confident, obedient, comfortable working with people and used to different environments.

Training an assistance animal

Training takes time and effort, even with specially bred animals from organizations such as Guide Dogs for the Blind and Dogs for Good. Puppies first need to be 'socialized', living with puppy-walkers for a time to let them get used to family life and become house-trained and obedient. During this period they will become familiar with different environments from busy city streets to parks and buses and will come into contact with different people and other animals.

After about a year, the dog will begin its specialized training at a training centre. Exactly what is taught will depend on the disability. For instance, a hearing dog learns how to alert a deaf person to a sound by touching him with its nose or paw and then leading him to the source of the sound, such as the front door or the telephone. In case of danger, the dogs are taught to lie down so that their owner knows that something is wrong. This might happen if, for instance, a smoke alarm is activated. Guide dogs for the blind spend about nine months with skilled instructors before completing their training with their new, blind owner, so that they become a team. The dogs learn to ignore distractions, avoid obstacles, stop at changes in ground level such as kerbs or steps, and lead their owner in a straight line. They must stop at the kerb and wait for the 'Forward' command, which the owner gives after listening to make sure no car is approaching. However, if it is not safe to cross and the owner has not heard an approaching car, the dog stays on the pavement. The training at Dogs for Good is similar, except that these animals must learn to walk next to a wheelchair, 'fetch' and retrieve dropped items such as a purse or a TV remote control, and bark for help if assistance is needed. They are then, at about 18 months to 2 years old, matched with an owner and their training continues together while the dog learns exactly what its new duties are. Opening and closing doors, shopping, turning lights on and off, operating pedestrian crossing buttons, helping their owner dress and undress, even loading and emptying the washing machine are all in a day's work for these amazing animals. The organization explains that Labradors, Retrievers and Cocker Spaniels are frequently chosen for the work as they are dogs which love to 'fetch' and carry, retrieve, and interact with people!

All assistance animals are carefully matched with their owners. An energetic young man will need a livelier assistance dog than an older person who goes out less frequently. The aim is to achieve a lifetime partnership. Assistance dogs usually 'retire' at the age of 10 or 11 and are then kept as family pets either by their former owner or by one of the many families who apply to re-home retired assistance dogs.

Hounds for Heroes

A specialist charity trains assistance dogs to help former members of the armed forces and the emergency services who have been injured or disabled. Hounds for Heroes began by raising £100,000 to pay for the training of five puppies. They now have puppies in both 'basic' and 'advanced' training at their base in Petersfield, Hampshire. Like other charities they are keen to hear from local, potential 'puppy parents' who train and socialize the young pups at home before they begin their training proper and are then matched with their ex-service partners. Like other assistance animals they are trained to do whatever is required, from posting letters and helping with shopping to taking money out of an ATM!

Medical Detection Dogs

Back in the 1980s, I interviewed a woman who claimed that her dog had identified a cancerous mole on the back of her thigh. It sounded extraordinary. Her dog was an ordinary family pet which had made a point of worrying at the mole every time the owner wore shorts or a short skirt. The little mongrel made such a fuss that the woman eventually went to her doctor and was referred to a dermatologist, who confirmed that the mole was indeed cancerous. At that time, little research was done into dogs' ability to 'sniff out' illness or malignancy. It all seemed a bit too far-fetched. However, research has moved on since then and the charity Medical Detection Dogs was set up in 2008.

There are two branches in this organization. One of them trains dogs to help people manage complex health conditions such as diabetes. A dog's sense of smell is extremely sensitive, perhaps 200 times more sensitive than a human's. This is why dogs are trained to sniff out drugs and other contraband by the police and customs officers. Researchers have now discovered that dogs can identify odour changes associated with some of the most common problems linked to diabetes control, including the so-called 'hypo' which occurs when blood-sugar levels go too low, causing dizziness, sweating, trembling and loss of concentration. When a trained dog becomes aware there is something wrong, it can then alert the owner by jumping up or licking him, get help, and even fetch medical supplies, glucose tablets or a sweet fizzy drink.

Holly the Whippet was the winner of the 'Caring Animal of the Year' award at the *Daily Mirror*'s 'Animal Heroes' ceremony in 2015. Holly had been rescued from a so-called 'puppy farm' where she had been used for breeding. When she was re-homed with teenager Amy Wilton, she was painfully skinny and frightened, with rotten teeth. Amy nursed her back to health and was rewarded by Holly sensing when Amy, who is diabetic, was experiencing dangerously low blood-sugar levels.

'Holly is a one-person dog and she attached herself to me from the start,' Amy says. 'If I go out, she sits waiting by the door; if I have a shower, she presses her nose against the screen. Then one night she woke me by jumping on my bed. I thought she wanted to go out but she refused to go. Instead she jumped up and put her paws on my shoulders. I realized I felt dizzy and unwell and when I did a blood test I realized Holly must be warning me! At first I thought it was coincidence – she hadn't been trained as a medical detection dog – but it happened a few more times. Since then, she must have warned me a hundred times. She seems to be able to smell the hormone and perspiration changes which accompany a diabetic 'hypo' some time before I am aware of any symptoms. She has probably saved my life on more than one occasion. Holly is my shadow, part of me, and I love her to pieces.'

'Alert' dogs can be trained to help with other conditions as well as diabetes, for example crises in Addison's disease (a disorder of the adrenal glands causing dehydration, weakness, headache and shallow breathing), narcolepsy (a condition in which patients fall asleep with no warning) or severe allergic reactions. Research into other conditions which might be helped by a canine 'warning light' is continuing. Most dogs are specially trained, although the charity says that they are approached by people whose pet seems already to be trying to 'alert' them to something going wrong, and that a pet with the right temperament can also become a detection dog.

Medical detection dogs are also involved in cancer diagnosis, especially in the case of those cancers which are otherwise difficult to diagnose reliably. Cancer diagnosis and treatment is improving all the time. Most of us are aware now that early diagnosis gives patients a much better chance of a successful outcome. It seems that dogs might be able to help with this. The medical journal *Gut* reported in 2011 that a trained 'detection dog' was successfully able to detect 33 out of 37 cancers from breath or stool samples. It is now known that some sort of 'cancer scent' exists and that dogs can sniff it out, although we don't yet know which actual chemical compounds might be involved. It seems that, as well as skin cancers, dogs have been successful in sniffing out bladder, lung, breast, ovarian and colon tumours, whether the malignancy was at a very early stage or was more advanced. Experiments to discover this were very carefully set up so that the humans watching didn't know which samples were malignant and couldn't, therefore, 'cue' the dog in any way! However, there do seem to be problems in moving this research forward and using dogs routinely to diagnose cancer, because the ability to sniff it out does vary between different animals and also in the same dog on different days. There have even been reports that Japanese researchers have tried to devise a kind of electronic 'dog's nose' . . .

Even more intriguingly, in the autumn of 2015 the magazine *Your Cat* reported a case of a woman whose elderly moggy suddenly began tapping the back of her neck and miaowing loudly. She had previously noticed a painless lump on her neck but had ignored it. Eventually, when the cat continued to paw at the area, she went to her GP. A few days later she was diagnosed with Hodgkin's lymphoma, which had already reached an advanced stage. She credits her cat with saving her life – and the magazine found cases in the USA of cats whose odd behaviour had led to similar incidents.

Ever since the late 1980s there has been anecdotal evidence that dogs can also somehow sense if their owner is going to have an epileptic seizure, although actual documentary evidence is hard to come by. The organization Support Dogs, founded in 1992 and based in Sheffield, has found that dogs can give people with epilepsy a reliable 50-minute warning that they may have a seizure. This gives the owner time to get him- or herself to a safe place, and means that those with epilepsy, including the 30 per cent whose condition is poorly controlled by medication, can feel more confident about going out, cooking, having a bath and leading a normal life.

Toni Brown-Griffin from Kent has had epileptic seizures since her late teens. In her early 20s she had a severe asthma attack resulting in an increase in seizures and an eight-week hospital stay.

'When I returned home I was having at least 12 seizures a week,' she says. 'I was a regular visitor to A&E with falls, lacerations and broken bones. I lost my job and my driving licence and the strong drugs I took weren't effective.

'I'd always been an animal-lover, and one of my dogs, a rescue Collie, seemed to pay especial attention to me when I had a seizure so I contacted the National Epilepsy Society who sent me a leaflet about support dogs. Rupert was only the second dog they trained. I now have Hetty, who is actually a trained guide dog as well as a seizure alert dog, as I am blind as well.

'Hetty means everything to me. I don't know what I would do without her. Her training was similar to that of a guide dog. With these dogs, it's not about their breed or size, it's about their temperament. They have to want to be with you at all times and that's what Hetty is like. If I get up, she gets up. If I go to the loo and don't come back soon, she will come to fetch me.

'We don't yet know exactly how seizure alert dogs know what's happening. Researchers believe they are able to sense a lot of minute physical and biological changes in their owners. If Hetty is guiding, in her harness, and she senses that I am going to have a seizure, she will pull over in front of me, stare at my face, and rest her head on my left knee. If she then touches me with her paw I know I will have a major seizure in 42 minutes. If she doesn't touch me with her paw, I know I have 15 minutes before I have a minor seizure.

'I have lots of pets but I feel Hetty is just phenomenal. Without her my life would be so restricted. She is always looking out for me and I know how lucky I am to have her.'

Dementia dogs

There is increasing concern about the country's ageing population and the problems caused by the numbers of people living with dementia. Could assistance dogs really help with this distressing condition too? The world's first 'dementia dogs' project was set up in partnership with Alzheimer Scotland in 2013. Oscar, a Golden Retriever, and Kaspa, a Labrador, both of whom came from the guide dogs breeding programme, were 'matched' with their families not long afterwards and have been a great success. As well as providing company for couples where one partner is affected by Alzheimer's, the dogs have been trained to alert their owners to switch the oven on and off, take their medication on time, and generally maintain a healthy routine. Having an assistance dog can help someone with dementia to stay active, improve her confidence, and calm her down when the dog senses that she is becoming upset and agitated.

In other countries, dogs are trained to help those with mental as well as physical health issues. And, of course, the ability of dogs – and other animals – to connect on many levels with children who have conditions like autism has already been established in this country and overseas. We shall be looking at just what animals can do for children, including those with special needs, in Chapter 6.

6

Animals and children

It's generally agreed that growing up with animals is good for children. As well as providing love and companionship, having a pet in the house teaches children responsibility. Dogs have to be walked, cats, rabbits, guinea pigs and hamsters have to be fed, watered and cleaned out. An animal is not a toy which can be discarded when the owner is bored with it. If your child is clamouring for a pet and you are wondering whether a pet would fit in with your lifestyle, how can you be sure you're doing the right thing?

It's a good idea to take advice from one of the many animal charities which re-home unwanted and abandoned pets, all of which are dedicated to finding exactly the right owners for the animals in their care. Not all rescue centres will re-home animals to families with babies and toddlers. This isn't because the pet may be a threat to the child – rather the reverse! Young kittens' and puppies' bones are soft and easily damaged by over-enthusiastic or rough handling. Small children – indeed, *all* children – need to learn to respect animals and treat them gently. They also need to know that animals which are teased and tormented will scratch and bite.

Good centres 'match' animals with their potential families very carefully. Cats Protection say that they will home suitable cats to families with 'respectful children'. Battersea Dogs and Cats Home say that all their animals are individually assessed to find out what they are like and what sort of home they need. Is this cat or dog a family pet, would it settle well with older rather than younger children, or does it need an adult-only home? The Mayhew Animal Home say that they are happy to re-home to families with young children providing the animal has been assessed as suitable and the parents will teach the children how to respect and treat animals. The Blue Cross also make the point that some 'small furries' such as hamsters and chinchillas are basically nocturnal, so may very well be sleeping when children want to play with them. They also say that rabbits and other smaller animals don't always appreciate being picked up and cuddled.

Providing your family chooses the right pet and you all take the responsibility of pet ownership seriously, including the children, having an animal or animals in your life can prove enormously rewarding in so many ways. There are many advantages to having pets in the family; for example,

- Having a pet teaches children about empathy, loyalty and respect for other creatures. The dog still has to be walked even when the child is tired and would rather phone a friend or play on the Xbox!
- Having a pet teaches children about life. They may experience a birth in the family and learn how to care for tiny, vulnerable newborns as well as learning to cope with death and grieving when – as is almost inevitable – they lose a much-loved pet.
- Children learn nurturing skills as well as responsibility. They may save their pocket money for treats for Fluffy or Rover.
- They learn how to handle a different species appropriately and how to look for signs that things are not quite right if the pet becomes ill.
- Like adult pet owners, they are rewarded with unconditional love and friendship. Many children say that their dog or cat is their best friend and confidante.

Research suggests that children growing up with pets have higher self-esteem and improved social skills, better attention spans, better school attendance and more emotional stability. A research study from Cambridge University in May 2015, which had looked at interactions between children and pets over ten years, concluded that we tend to underestimate the importance of pets to children. Many confide in their pets when they are going through difficult experiences such as parental divorce or bereavement.

Pets and children's health

There is no reason to suppose that having a well-cared-for pet in the home will pose any threat to children's health, providing sensible hygiene precautions are taken. The NHS Choices website

(<nhs.uk> and type 'Choices' into the search box) says that it's rare for infections to be passed from animals to children. Conditions which can occur include ringworm (a skin infection), toxocariasis (caused by worms found in cat or dog poo) and toxoplasmosis (caused by a parasite found in cat poo as well as undercooked or infected meat). It's important to remember to

- wash your hands after touching animals, being particularly careful to do so before preparing food;
- make sure your children wash their hands too, wiping them with anti-bacterial wipes if necessary;
- keep children away from litter trays and animal droppings in parks and fields;
- make sure your pets are vaccinated and treated for worms and fleas;
- keep pets away from food preparation areas in the kitchen;
- keep pets' dishes and cutlery separate from the family's.

Allergies

As we saw in Chapter 2, there has been a big rise in childhood allergies in the last 50 years, the causes of which are not known. According to Allergy UK, pets are a major cause of allergic disease and 50 per cent of allergic children are sensitive to cat allergens – normally 'dander', which is a mixture of hair and saliva. If your child has an allergy, clearly having a furry or feathered pet in the house is inappropriate. However, there are many studies which suggest that for children *without* a history of allergies, growing up with pets can actually have a protective effect.

A large research study from Sweden, published in November 2015, found that having a dog in the family in the first year of life actually reduces a child's risk of asthma by 15 per cent, and that contact with farm animals may actually halve this risk! This was a large study looking at a million children born in Sweden between 2001 and 2010. However, the authors say they don't know how this protective effect actually works, and the charity Asthma UK says that more research is needed.

Animals and learning

Most children are fascinated by animals and pets and many schools have introduced animals into the learning environment with great success. A report from the Society for Companion Animal Studies (SCAS) describes the advantages to children of animals in the classroom. Not only do they learn about caring for different animals, but animals can also be used in the curriculum to teach children about science and health and encourage their interest in art by producing drawings, paintings, poems and stories. Children who are not able to have a pet at home are able to share in animal care at school.

The Pets as Therapy (PAT) organization also runs a scheme called Read2Dogs, in which suitable dogs come into the classroom at intervals to be a 'listening ear' for children who find it easier to practise reading to a friendly pooch than to a teacher or parent.

'We launched the Read2Dogs scheme in 2011,' says PAT's Dinah Baynton-Dibley.

> Those working with therapy dogs in the USA noticed that introducing dogs into schools motivated the children – even those who were reluctant readers or perhaps had behavioural issues. We began forming links with interested local schools and PAT volunteers went in once a week with their dogs for an hour. Teachers identified the children they thought would benefit and set up a quiet reading area for individual children or small groups. The scheme is amazingly successful with some children, increasing their reading age by two years in a single term! Being with the dog removes all the stress of having to read in front of their peers. There is no judgement, no teasing, just a calm and relaxing experience, reading while they stroke a friendly dog. The scheme breaks down barriers and helps the children in both mainstream and special-needs schools to learn without realizing it!

An Australian study in the 1990s found that including a cat in primary-school classrooms encouraged the children to be calmer, quieter and more co-operative. The SCAS can offer teachers advice and help on the best way to plan the introduction of a school pet, care for it and make sure the children benefit from the interaction with the animal or animals.

Children with special needs

Many children with special needs seem to bond more easily with animals than they do with people. Cats Protection's 'Cat of the Year' in 2012 was Jessi-Cat, who belongs to the Dillon family of Manchester. Young Lorcan Dillon, who is now 11, has a social anxiety disorder called 'selective mutism' which prevented him from speaking in certain situations – for example, in school or in front of strangers. He also has Asperger's, an autistic spectrum disorder which affects the way he relates to other people. When Jessi-Cat came into his life, she transformed it and the two became inseparable, with Lorcan managing to tell Jessi that he loved her and that she was his best friend. His mother Jayne wrote a book, *Jessi-Cat: The story of a cat that unlocked a boy's heart*, detailing the difference the bond between Lorcan and his pet has made.

'We never imagined that Lorcan would be so gentle and protective with Jessi,' says Jayne.

> Somehow picking her up and cuddling her helped him to express his emotions. She is an extraordinary cat – very placid, but extremely vocal, so that when Lorcan speaks to her, she miaows right back, and that seemed to help his speech! He is popular at school and has been in the Cub Scouts, and is beginning to find it easier to understand other people's point of view. Getting Jessi-Cat was the best thing we ever did for Lorcan!

There are many other examples of bonding between children with autistic spectrum disorders and animals. One Australian research study found that introducing dogs to these children could actually reduce the levels of cortisol – one of the fight-or-flight hormones – in their bodies. Schools for children with special needs often have a dog as an extra staff member!

> The Ian Mikardo High School in east London is attended by students who have been excluded from mainstream education – often from several schools. The learning environment is deliberately designed to be 'different' so that it doesn't feel school-like, and the presence of rescue Border Collie McFlurry is part of that. The school's 'mission statement' says:
>
> > Regular contact with animals has been shown to make children calmer, better able to concentrate and co-operate. A well-trained

and good-tempered dog can help modify disruptive behaviour, reduce friction and increase attendance.

For many of our students, the school's dog is their first healthy relationship. For a boy who has had difficulty engaging with human beings, and who has experienced multiple rejections, to be able to stroke a dog or walk with him through the grounds is a sign of acceptance.

McFlurry's presence makes the Head Teacher's office a welcoming place, and students can be helped to learn relationship skills by learning to care for the dog. He was a rescue himself and had six previous homes before being adopted by the Head Teacher. Of course, engaging with the dog is not forced on students who for health or cultural reasons are unwilling. But McFlurry plays a significant part in the fun and laughter at our school and loves to join in with the football!

The organization Dogs for Good can provide 'autism assistance dogs' which are specially trained, like guide dogs. They help children aged between 3 and 10 who have been diagnosed with autism. They wear a special harness attaching them to the child and parent or carer. Walking alongside the dog helps the child to relax in what may be an unfamiliar situation and also prevents the child from running off. The dog is trained to 'sit' if the child tries to run away. These dogs have all the rights of other assistance dogs like guide dogs for the blind.

Dogs for Good also run a PAWS Family Dog Service offering information and support to families wanting to choose and train a pet dog to benefit their family. Pet dogs can be very beneficial but don't have the full rights of an assistance animal.

A three-year joint project between Dogs for Good, the National Autistic Society and Lincoln University found that owning a pet dog reduced stress in both autistic children and their parents. In the study, 85 per cent of the parents reported their child was happier, 62 per cent said their child was less likely to have a 'meltdown', and 69 per cent found that their own stress levels were reduced after as little as six weeks.

Equine therapy

We saw in Chapter 2 that contact with horses can be extremely therapeutic and there are Riding for the Disabled groups all over the country, offering children as well as adults with special needs the chance to ride and care for horses and ponies. The Wormwood Scrubs Pony Centre in London was founded in 1989 with just three ponies and now has 20, plus a team of trained instructors and volunteers. Children with both physical and learning disabilities can learn to ride and also enjoy 'Grooming Time': and 'One With' bonding sessions.

'We see children with a wide range of problems,' says Projects Manager Bee Pike.

> Some have autism, some have cerebral palsy, some have behavioural problems and/or come from disadvantaged backgrounds. Some actually ride the horses and ponies, some groom them, some simply interact, using all their senses in 'Paint-a-Pony' sessions where they use the animal as a canvas and actually paint them, using their hands and safe paint.
>
> Our work benefits all kinds of children. They might learn to smile, or non-verbal children might talk to the horses even if they can't talk to people. We had one little lad who was frightened and screamed at first, but gradually got used to the horses until he loved coming so much he was always first on the bus! We can see the children's confidence grow, both on and off the horses, and their behaviour improves at school and in care centres too. Children who weren't willing – or able – to concentrate, or focus on their lessons, may do so if they know they're coming to us later. We see teenage boys who can be a bit mouthy and know-it-all react in a different way. Horses are large animals and they learn they *have* to 'ask nicely' or the horse will not respond. Once they have learned to say thank you to the horse and the team leader, they do the same at school and at home.
>
> Horses are sentient creatures who allow the children to communicate with them. Our horses definitely tune in to special-needs children and are totally aware of what they are doing!

Donkey therapy

Most animal lovers will have at least heard of the Donkey Sanctuary in Sidmouth, Devon, which was founded back in 1969 as a refuge and rescue centre for unwanted, abused and abandoned donkeys.

Less well known is the fact that the Sanctuary has been providing 'donkey therapy' – mostly to children but also to old people in care and nursing homes and hospices – for almost as long as it has been in existence. They currently provide about 50,000 donkey-assisted therapy sessions every year, not just in Sidmouth but also in Belfast, Birmingham, Ivybridge, Leeds and Manchester.

'Our founder, Dr Elisabeth Svendsen, was a pioneer in the area of animal-assisted therapy,' explains spokeswoman Suzi Cretney.

As well as loving donkeys, she had a background in special-needs teaching and knew that children have a natural affinity with animals, and one that can be brought out if they are enabled to interact with quiet and easy-going creatures such as donkeys. Her work began in the 1970s.

Donkeys are quite different from horses, and children, especially those who are young and nervous, react differently to them. They are less fidgety and much more relaxed as well as being smaller. Even children who struggle to communicate are happy with donkeys. We work with all kinds of children including those with profound disabilities, behavioural difficulties, social problems and conditions like autism, and we tailor our sessions to the individual child. We see groups of schoolchildren and also support groups for Down's Syndrome children. We also run a Saturday club for special-needs children and their siblings so that no-one is left out and everyone can experience the donkeys in their own way.

The benefits for the children can be really profound. We have had children with selective mutism whose first words were spoken to one of our donkeys. Often it's the quiet moments that matter. We run caring and grooming programmes so that the children begin to understand the donkeys' needs too. The connection between children and donkeys is a powerful one.

Interestingly, Suzi says that the therapy benefits the donkeys just as much as it does the children!

'We are an animal welfare organization first and foremost,' she says.

Our donkeys come here from all kinds of backgrounds. Not all of them are retired. Some, especially the younger ones, *want* to work and get as much out of the sessions as the children do. We select the donkeys carefully – a groom will tell us when there is one which is happy with children, and then it goes along to the centre for therapy sessions.

We also take donkeys into care homes and hospices and, again, it's amazing to see the connection with older people who may previously have been entirely passive. Many come from a generation which grew up knowing about beach donkeys . . . so there are lots of different outcomes by introducing people to donkeys!

Dolphin therapy

Swimming with dolphins is an item on many peoples' 'bucket list' and there are facilities around the world which offer it as a holiday experience, but it can be more than that. Dolphins are highly intelligent animals: self-aware, able to communicate with one another, although we don't really know how they do this. Some people believe that they can actually sense areas of trauma or disability in the human body, although the evidence for this is mostly anecdotal. Back in the 1970s, an American educational anthropologist noted the interaction between her disabled brother and dolphins, and doctors in Florida developed what became known as 'dolphin-assisted therapy' from there.

Dolphins have their own natural 'sonar' and emit ultrasound waves in order to communicate, and it was thought that this might, in some way, be able to modify human brainwave activity. Children with Down's Syndrome were said to benefit from this form of therapy and even today there are facilities, in the USA and other parts of the world, where 'dolphin-assisted therapy' can be experienced.

However, it is an extremely controversial form of therapy and most animal welfare groups say that as the benefits are as yet unproven and dolphins do not thrive in captivity, it is morally wrong to use these amazing creatures in this way. In the wild, dolphins live in complex social groups known as 'pods' and use their 'sonar' – known as echolocation – to explore the ocean environment. Separating individual animals from their pods is as cruel as separating children from their families. Responsible tourist organizations may offer an opportunity to view – or even swim with – wild dolphins in their natural habitat but point out that these are large, strong creatures and their behaviour when they come into contact with humans can be unpredictable.

The Born Free Foundation's Zoo Check website says:

> There is *no* conclusive evidence that dolphin-assisted therapy (DAT) is any more effective than animal-assisted therapy with domestic animals such as dogs. The DAT industry is unregulated and offers hope to already vulnerable patients at the expense of the captive dolphins used in DAT programmes.

PAT dogs and students

It isn't just young children, or those with special needs, who can benefit from animal therapy. In the spring of 2014 six PAT dogs visited the University of East Anglia at the invitation of the Dean of Students, who said, 'We hope to provide a therapeutic medium for the recovery of self-esteem, to help lonely and depressed students feel less isolated, and enhance the well-being of vulnerable students.'

Seventy-seven per cent of the students said that the dogs' visit left them feeling happier, more cheerful and in a better mood overall, and 80 per cent said they felt less stressed.

7

Pet therapy and you

If you think that you – and your family – would benefit from having a pet in your life, how can you be sure that you choose the right animal? Sadly, rescue centres and charities are full of abandoned pets, sometimes given up for understandable reasons and with great regret, but at other times simply 'dumped' because the owners realized too late that they hadn't thought the issue through. In spite of the advertisements about a dog being for life and not just for Christmas, people still buy animals as presents, or on impulse – with the inevitable results.

Obviously, it's impossible to know for certain what will happen to you over the next 10 or 15 years – the lifespan of your companion animal – but before adopting, you should be as sure as you can be that you are offering your new companion a 'forever' home.

Choosing the right pet

A pet that will share and enrich your life needs to fit in with the way you live, with your environment, circumstances and personality. Do you work long hours, so that your pet will spend much of its time alone? Are you the outdoor type, or someone who likes to spend your leisure time on the sofa watching TV? Do you have a garden? Do you travel a lot? Do you live in the depths of the country, in a high-rise flat, on a busy suburban street? And – not least – can you afford to feed your pet, pay for its toys, insurance, veterinary care?

Here are some further points to consider:

- Having a puppy in your home is rather like adopting a toddler. It may cry in the night, chew items left lying around, and will definitely need toilet training and probably puppy obedience classes too.

- Are you particularly house-proud? Even the best-trained animals (dogs, cats, house rabbits) have the occasional 'accident'. Cats may claw the furniture, knock over delicate ornaments, shed fur everywhere, and leave 'presents' of half-eaten small rodents on your kitchen floor. Muddy paws inevitably make a mess. Bird and small animal cages need a lot of cleaning out.
- Having an animal means that spontaneous outings and weekends away are often not possible. Unless you have a reliable cat-feeder or dog-walker on hand, you can't just take off when you feel like it: the animals always have to be provided for.
- If you live with your family or with friends, are they as enthusiastic about getting an animal as you are? Is anyone in the household allergic to furry or feathered creatures? If you are renting your home, does your landlord allow pets?
- Are you planning to become pregnant any time soon? Many pets are given up because the owner decides to start a (human) family. It's perfectly possible to combine pregnancy and the care of a young baby with having a pet, but it is something to think about.
- What sort of relationship do you expect to have with your future pet? Do you want something cuddly? A lively dog to jog round the park with you and play Frisbee? A more unusual pet such as a rat, a ferret or a degu, which will be a talking point? Something interesting and unusual which you need to study, such as a snake, iguana or a tank of exotic tropical fish, which is as much of a hobby as a companion?
- Don't be influenced by fashion. The *Ninja Turtles* craze led to the abandoning of lots of unwanted terrapins – and is it *really* a good idea to contemplate keeping a Vietnamese pot-bellied pig in a suburban garden?

Choosing your pet

Once you have given some thought to the kind of animal you want to adopt, you can't do better than take advice from some of the many animal charities. Take a look at the websites of the PDSA, Blue Cross, Wood Green: The Animals Charity, Cats Protection or the Dogs Trust, which are a mine of information and will help you decide which animal is right for you. They all advise prospective pet owners *not* to buy on impulse (however cute the puppy in the pet-shop window) but to do plenty of research first so that you are as sure as you can be that you have chosen wisely. They also recommend that *you should never buy an animal from a random advertisement on the Internet*. Sadly, some unscrupulous people see animals as a commodity like any other, a way of making a quick profit, and allow their animals to have litter after litter with no regard for their welfare. Often, such animals are sold on before they are old enough to leave their mum, and the result is heartbreak with sickly, fading kittens and 'farmed' puppies – an appalling trade that needs to be stamped out.

The choice is often between a pedigree animal or a 'rescue' from a local shelter or somewhere like Battersea Dogs and Cats Home. If you opt for a pedigree animal, only buy from a reputable breeder. Make sure you see the kittens or puppies with their mother. The breeder should be able to show you the right paperwork, including Kennel Club registration, health certificates and a record of your chosen animal's worming and vaccinations. You could ask to speak to an owner who has obtained a pup or kitten from this same breeder, to be on the safe side. People who really care about their animals will be happy for you to do this. If they're not, avoid them and go elsewhere.

Animal rescue organizations always have lots and lots of kittens and puppies, cats and dogs, looking for their forever homes. Some like Wood Green: The Animals Charity re-home other animals too, from field animals such as pigs and goats to rescued battery chickens! If you are really set on adopting a particular breed of cat or dog, there are specialist rescue centres which re-home pedigree animals, such as Persian cats or retired racing greyhounds.

Another consideration is whether you want a young animal, which you will inevitably have to train and socialize, or a more mature pet whose character and personality is already established. It's your choice, of course, but you do need to remember that youngsters can be hard work! If you lead a quiet life yourself you may feel that a boisterous puppy or a kitten which climbs up the curtains is not the right pet for you. Older pets are generally more sensible. Rescue centres such as the Mayhew Animal Home in north-west London can always tell you about your chosen pet – its habits, its tastes, how much exercise it needs, how well it mixes with people, other animals, children and strangers – so that you can decide whether or not a particular animal is right for you. You can also expect a 'home visit' so that the rescue centre can assess you, your family and your environment. They are looking for 'forever homes' and don't want an animal placed with you to be returned as unsuitable.

The right pet for you is likely to be out there somewhere! Most charities like to place animals in homes with gardens, but there are some cats, for example, which are elderly, have always lived indoors or have a medical condition which means they are better as indoor cats. If you're worried about the risk of your cat getting run over and you have a garden, it's possible to 'cat-proof' it or build a safe run outside so that your cat can explore in safety. Animals kept indoors need lots of toys and stimulation or they can get bored and destructive. Rabbits and guinea pigs should not be confined to small cages; they need a good-sized outdoor run as well.

Think, too, about your pet's likely lifespan. Better vet care means that animals, like people, are living longer these days. It's not that unusual for cats to live into their late teens or early 20s. Guinea pigs are likely to live to between 5 and 8. Mice are 'elderly' at about 2 while parrots can live as long as 60 years (and are also likely to bond with one member of a family in particular), which is something to bear in mind. It really is important to do as much research as possible before taking on a pet of any kind.

Most rescue organizations neuter all their animals before re-homing them and many also ensure that the animals are microchipped so that they can be returned to you if they go missing. If you adopt an animal which is not neutered, it's essential to make sure this is done before your pet is old enough to reproduce. Vet fees for neutering are cheap and many charities do it for free. There are already far more animals than homes available and one unneutered female cat, for instance, can be responsible for 20,000 descendants in just five years if her kittens then have kittens! Don't take chances. It isn't true that cats 'need to have one litter first' – they don't! And unneutered male cats spray, fight (risking infections) and wander looking for females, putting themselves at risk of road accidents. Always neuter your pets!

If you think you would benefit from an assistance animal . . .

We saw in Chapter 5 how assistance animals can transform the lives of both children and adults with disabilities. If you are interested in having one, you need to contact the appropriate organization (contact details on pp. 61–3) to find out whether you are eligible and how long you might have to wait. Because there often are lengthy waiting lists, it is always worth registering your interest so that you can be informed as animals are trained.

Organizations providing assistance dogs all have their own eligibility criteria, which you need to check carefully as they may not be exactly what you expect! For example, you can have a guide dog if you still have some residual sight, whereas you are only eligible for a hearing dog if you have severe or profound deafness in both ears. (Although, if your hearing loss is *not* severe or profound, you may be eligible for one of the organization's 'confidence and companionship' dogs.)

Guide dogs, for example, can work with adults of any age – there's no upper age limit – and sometimes with under-16s as well. You don't have to be completely blind and you will not be ruled out if you have other health issues as well as sight problems. All equipment is provided, as well as assistance with dog food and vet bills if necessary. Most guide dogs are Labradors, Retrievers or similar crossbreeds, but if you have an allergy other breeds are sometimes available.

Dogs for Depression don't provide trained dogs. Instead they encourage interested people to 'rescue' an unwanted animal from a charity or rescue centre. They say that knowing you have offered a loving home to a dog who needs one can lift your spirits right from the start! Their tips for choosing the right dog apply to everyone taking on a pet and they recommend thinking carefully about the kind of dog who would fit in best with your family and lifestyle, and taking advice from the rescue centre about the right dog for you.

Canine Partners link people with physical disabilities – including former service personnel – with assistance dogs. In order to be accepted you'll need to be 18 or over. Those affected by multiple sclerosis, cerebral palsy, spinal and head injuries, brittle bones and many other conditions are eligible for a canine partner. You'll need to be willing to exercise the dog – with help if necessary – and provide it with a safe toileting area. The organization estimates that food will cost you £40 a month and insurance £25 a month. You also need to budget for worm and flea treatments at around £90 a year. Canine Partners are happy to discuss financial issues with prospective owners and point out that registered disabled people may get council help.

Hearing Dogs for Deaf People: to be eligible for a hearing dog, as we have seen, you need to be severely or profoundly deaf. You don't need to have owned a dog before but you need to promise to walk the dog for at least an hour every day, and not be away from it for more than four hours at a time. The organization also says that you should not have any other pet dogs under 8 years old. If you have an older pet, it will need to be assessed before you are teamed up with your hearing dog. There is a great demand for hearing dogs and you might find you have to wait as long as two or three years.

Support Dogs work with wheelchair users and autistic children. At the time of writing their waiting lists were closed but it is always worthwhile registering your interest as the situation changes and more animals are trained. The organization also works with 'seizure alert dogs' for people with epilepsy. To be eligible, you need to have been diagnosed with epilepsy and have at least ten seizures a month. You have to be over 16 and keep a 'seizure diary'. Only one member of your household should have epilepsy and your support dog should be the only dog in the household. Also, obviously, you need to love dogs and want to form a bond with your canine companion!

Medical Detection Dogs support people with life-threatening health conditions such as diabetes. Again, there is a waiting list of 18 months to three years. The charity says that in some circumstances it is possible to train your own pet dog as a medical detection dog –

for example, if your dog has already shown signs that it 'knows' when you are ill or about to be ill. Suitable dogs need to be people-orientated with a good sense of smell.

Dogs for Good provide assistance dogs for adults and children with disabilities, including autism. Again, their waiting lists are currently closed but it is worth registering your interest. Their PAWS 'Family Dog Project' runs workshops for families with autistic children, helping them to get the most out of their relationship with their family pet. Check their website for details of forthcoming workshops.

Useful addresses

Some of the organizations listed have telephone contact numbers. If these are not listed, the organization can be contacted via the website.

Alzheimer Scotland
24-hour Dementia Helpline (Freephone): 0808 808 3000
Website: www.alzscot.org

Battersea Dogs and Cats Home
Tel.: 0843 509 4444
Website: www.battersea.org.uk

Blue Cross
Tel. (supporter care team): 0300 790 9903
Website: www.bluecross.org.uk

Canine Partners
Website: http://caninepartners.org.uk

Care Farms
Tel. (Development Co-ordinators): 0300 600 0290
Website: www.carefarminguk.org

Cats Protection
Website: www.cats.org.uk

Cinnamon Trust
Tel.: 01736 757 900
Website: www.cinnamon.org.uk

Dog A.I.D. (Assistance in Disability)
Tel.: 01743 588 469
Website: www.dogaid.org.uk

Dogs for Depression
Website: http://dogsfordepression.org.uk

Dogs for Good
Tel.: 01295 252 600
Website: www.dogsforgood.org

Dogs Trust
Tel.: 0207 837 0006
Website: www.dogstrust.org.uk

Donkey Sanctuary
Tel.: 01395 578 222
Website: www.thedonkeysanctuary.org.uk

Guide Dogs for the Blind
Tel.: 0118 983 5555
Website: www.guidedogs.org.uk

Hearing Dogs for Deaf People
Tel.: 01844 348 100
Website: www.hearingdogs.org.uk

Henpower
Tel.: 0191 477 5775
Website: https:.//equalarts.org.uk

Hounds for Heroes
Tel.: 01730 823 118
Website: http://houndsforheroes.com

LEAP
Tel.: 0776 0776 500
Website: www.leapequine.com

Mayhew Animal Home
Tel.: 0208 962 8000
Website: https://themayhew.org

Medical Detection Dogs
Tel.: 01296 655 888
Website: www.medicaldetectiondogs.org.uk

Mental Health Foundation
Tel.: 020 7803 1100
Website: www.mentalhealth.org.uk

National Animal Welfare Trust
Tel.: 0208 950 0177
Website: www.nawt.org.uk

Our Special Friends
Tel.: 0300 030 9940
Website: www.ourspecialfriends.com

People and Pets Advocates
Tel.: 0300 666 3999
Website: www.papas.org.uk

PDSA
Tel.: 0800 731 2502
Website: www.pdsa.org.uk

Pets as Therapy
Tel.: 01494 569 130
Website: http://petsastherapy.org

Riding for the Disabled
Tel.: 01926 492 915
Website: www.rda.org.uk

Sarah Urwin, counsellor and psychotherapist
Tel.: 01363 85154
Website: www.sarahurwin.co.uk

Sirona Therapeutic Horsemanship
Tel.: 07958 356 114 or 07818 453 402
Website: http://sironacic.com

Society for Companion Animal Studies
Tel.: 0845 601 2207
Website: www.scas.org.uk

Stroke Rehab Dogs
Tel.: 07543 202 434
Website: www.strokerehabdogs.co.uk

Support Dogs
Tel.: 0114 261 7800
Website: https://supportdogs.org.uk

Wings of Freedom
Tel: 07845 504 167
Website: http://wingsoffreedom.org.uk

Wood Green: The Animals Charity
Tel.: 0300 303 9333
Website: www.woodgreen.org.uk

References

Cinnamon Trust, *Pet Friendly Care Homes*, fourth edition (Hayle: Cinnamon Trust, 2013; available from 01736 757 900).

James Bowen, *A Street Cat Named Bob* (London: Hodder Paperbacks, 2012).

Jayne Dillon, *Jessi-Cat: The story of a cat that unlocked a boy's heart* (London: Michael O'Mara Books, 2013).

Jacki Gordon, *My Dog, My Friend* (Dorchester: Hubble & Hattie, 2014).

Index